T0128580

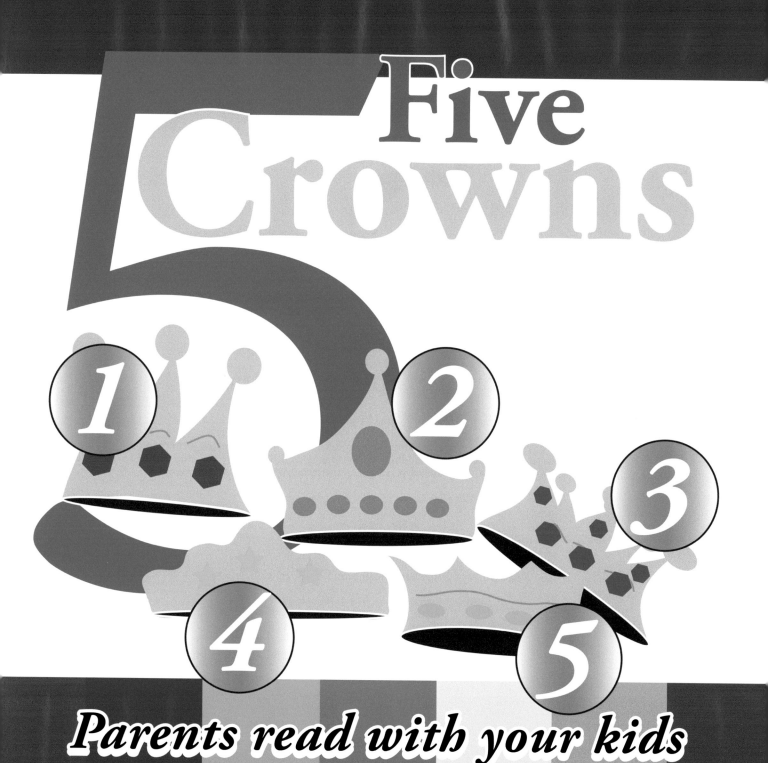

By Wilma Brumfield-Lofton
Illustrated by André Brumfield

To order additional copies of this book, contact:
Xlibris
1-888-795-4274
www.Xlibris.com
Orders@Xlibris.com

Library of Congress Control Number: 2020914513

ISBN: Softcover   978-1-7960-1527-0
       Hardcover   978-1-7960-1528-7
       EBook   978-1-7960-1526-3

Print information available on the last page.

Rev. date: 08/06/2020

GREATNESS

You are Crowned with
GREATNESS

This Book Belongs to:

_____

_____

_____

From: _____

Date: _____

London thinks she's a Princess. She has a crown that she wears at home all the time. She has worn it so much that it's starting to tarnish. Her dad always reads Bible Stories to her. Last night he read about the Five Crowns. Believers can receive these Crowns by living a righteous life.

This really caught London's attention…

The first Crown...

Crown of Righteousness

For those looking forward to the return of Christ.

2 Timothy 4:8

The second
Crown...

Incorruptible Crown

For those who have self- control and self discipline.

The third
Crown...

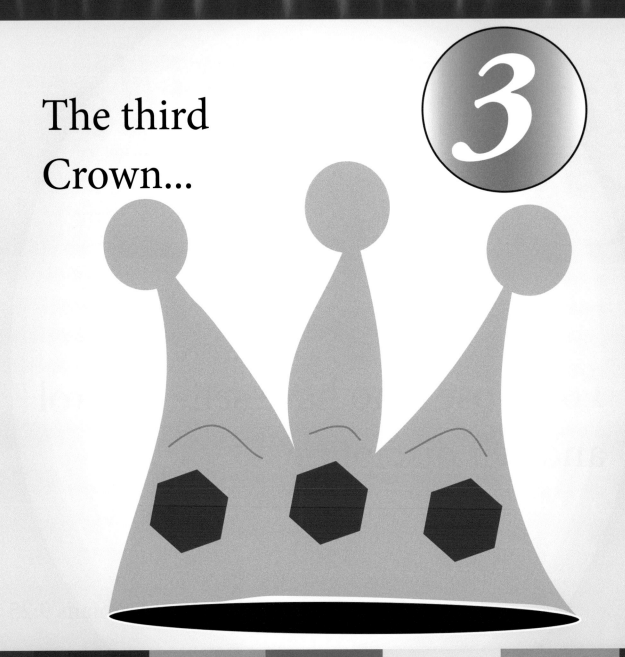

Crown of Life

For those who endured
patiently through trials.

James 1:12

The fourth
Crown...

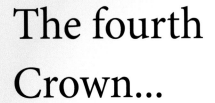

Crown of Glory

For those who teach the Good News of Christ.

1 Peter 5:1-4

The fifth
Crown...

Crown of Rejoicing

For those who lead others
to Christ.

1 Thessalonians 2:19

London was surprised and very happy to learn that by obeying God's word, believers will be Rewarded Crowns in Heaven. These Crowns will last forever and never rust, tarnish or fade away.

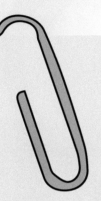

Note to: the parents

Parents give yourself a pat on the back. You are great parents and followers of Christ.

Proverbs 22:6
6 Train up a child in the way he should go;
even when he is old, he will not depart from it.

Deuteronomy 6:5-7
5 You shall love the Lord your God with all your heart and with all your soul and with all your might. 6 And these words that I command you today shall be on your heart. 7 You shall teach them diligently to your children, and shall talk of them when you sit in your house, and when you walk by the way, and when you lie down, and when you rise.

Fun Activities

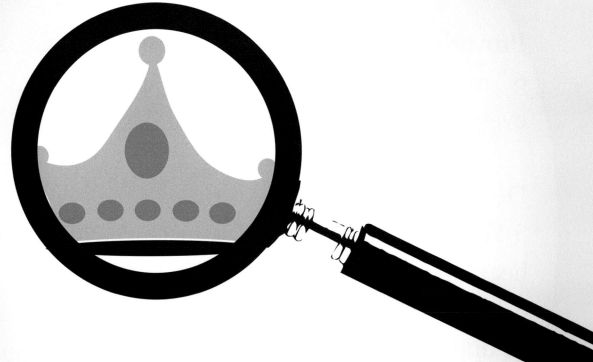

look real close

Which one is different?

Complete the pattern

Find the match

21

These crowns are among the rewards that God has for us. As believers we should live our lives in such a way, to be rewarded crowns, that will last forever and never fade away.

Printed in the United States
By Bookmasters